Android App Development: From Concept to Code

BY PRASUN BARUA

ABOUT

Welcome to "Android App Development: From Concept to Code"! This book serves as your gateway to the world of Android app development, offering a structured and in-depth exploration of the Android ecosystem. Whether you're a novice stepping into the world of app development or an experienced developer looking to refine your skills, this guide empowers you with the knowledge and practical expertise to create exceptional Android applications. Android, with its vast user base and diverse range of devices, presents enticing opportunities for developers. Its versatility and reach allow you to build innovative and impactful apps, whether it's a popular game, a productivity tool, or a niche-specific utility. We understand that learning can be challenging, and this book aims to make it smooth and rewarding. With practical examples, clear explanations, and a hands-on approach, we bridge the gap between theory and application. This book caters to a diverse audience, including beginners, intermediate developers, and experienced professionals. Beginners will appreciate the step-by-step guidance, while intermediate and experienced developers can explore advanced topics and refine their coding practices. Whether you follow the chapters sequentially or dive into specific sections that align with your needs, hands-on practice is essential. Each chapter includes practical examples and exercises to reinforce your learning through active coding. This comprehensive guide covers a wide range of topics, including setting up your development environment, designing user interfaces, handling user interactions, working with data, networking, security, optimizing performance, and much more. It also provides insights into publishing your app, monetization options, and testing and debugging strategies. As you embark on this Android app development journey, remember that it's not just about building apps; it's about creating meaningful experiences, solving real-world problems, and making a difference in users' lives. Embrace each chapter with curiosity, practice relentlessly, and view challenges as opportunities for growth. Happy coding!

TABLE OF CONTENTS

Handling Network Connectivity

Optimizing Memory and CPU Usage
Best Practices for App Performance

Building a Practical Android App from Scratch
Step-by-Step Code Walkthrough
Troubleshooting Common Issues

Handy Shortcuts and Techniques
Debugging Tips
Performance Optimization Tips

Key Android Development Terminology

CHAPTER 1: INTRODUCTION TO ANDROID APP DEVELOPMENT

1.1 Understanding the Android Ecosystem

Before diving into the world of Android app development, it's crucial to grasp the fundamentals of the Android ecosystem. Android is an open-source operating system primarily designed for mobile devices, but it's also used in various other forms, such as tablets, smart TVs, and even some laptops.

Key Concepts:

- **Android Operating System:** Android is based on the Linux kernel and is maintained by Google. It provides a rich platform for building mobile applications.
- **Android Versions:** Android is continuously evolving, with each version introducing new features and improvements. Developers need to understand the differences between various Android versions and how to target them.
- **Google Play Store:** This is the primary distribution platform for Android apps. Developers publish their apps on the Play Store, where users can download and install them.
- **Device Fragmentation:** Android runs on a wide range of devices with different screen sizes, resolutions, hardware capabilities, and Android

versions. Developers must consider this fragmentation when designing and testing their apps.

1.2 Why Develop for Android?

There are several compelling reasons to choose Android app development:

- **Market Share:** Android has the largest market share among mobile operating systems worldwide, making it a lucrative platform for app developers.
- **Open Source:** Android is open source, which means developers have access to the source code. This fosters innovation and allows for extensive customization.
- **Diverse User Base:** Android users come from diverse demographics and geographic locations, offering a broad audience for your apps.
- **Multiple Form Factors:** Android runs on various devices, including smartphones, tablets, smart TVs, and wearables. This diversity provides opportunities to create a wide range of applications.
- **Monetization:** Android apps can be monetized through various methods, such as in-app advertising, in-app purchases, and premium app sales.

1.3 Setting Up Your Development Environment

To start developing Android apps, you'll need to set up your development environment. Here's an overview of the essential steps:

1.3.1 Installing Android Studio:

- Android Studio is the official integrated development environment (IDE) for Android app development. It provides tools for designing, coding, and testing your apps.

1.3.2 Installing Java Development Kit (JDK):

- Android apps are primarily written in Java or Kotlin. Install the appropriate version of the JDK and configure it in Android Studio.

1.3.3 Android SDK and Emulator:

- The Android Software Development Kit (SDK) contains libraries, tools, and emulators necessary for app development. Android Studio can help you download and manage these components.

1.3.4 Creating Your First Project:

- Android Studio offers templates for various types of Android apps. You can choose a template and start a new project.

1.3.5 Device Setup:

- To test your apps, you can use physical Android devices or virtual devices (emulators). Android Studio allows you to configure and launch virtual devices with different configurations.

1.3.6 Understanding the Development Workflow:

- Familiarize yourself with the typical Android development workflow, which involves designing user interfaces, writing code, testing on different devices, and debugging.

Setting up your development environment correctly is the foundation of Android app development. Once your environment is ready, you can start building, testing, and refining your Android apps. Throughout this book, you will explore each aspect of Android app development in more detail, gaining practical experience and knowledge to create successful Android applications.

CHAPTER 2: GETTING STARTED WITH ANDROID STUDIO

2.1 Installing Android Studio

Android Studio is the official Integrated Development Environment (IDE) for Android app development. Installing Android Studio is the first step in your journey to becoming an Android app developer. Here's a detailed look at the installation process:

2.1.1 System Requirements: Before installing Android Studio, ensure that your computer meets the system requirements. These requirements may change with new versions, so it's essential to check the official documentation for the latest information.

2.1.2 Downloading Android Studio: Visit the official Android Studio download page on the Android Developer website (https://developer.android.com/studio) and download the version suitable for your operating system (Windows, macOS, or Linux).

2.1.3 Installation Steps: Once the download is complete, follow these steps to install Android Studio:

- **Windows:**
    - Run the downloaded installer (.exe file).
    - Follow the on-screen instructions to complete the installation.

- **macOS:**
    - o Open the downloaded .dmg file.
    - o Drag and drop the Android Studio icon into the Applications folder.
- **Linux:**
    - o Extract the downloaded .zip file to your desired location.
    - o Navigate to the extracted folder and run the "studio.sh" script to launch Android Studio.

2.1.4 Android SDK Setup: When you first launch Android Studio, it will prompt you to set up the Android Software Development Kit (SDK). This SDK contains essential libraries and tools required for Android app development. Android Studio will guide you through the installation process.

2.2 Exploring the IDE

After successfully installing Android Studio, it's essential to become familiar with the IDE's interface and key components:

2.2.1 Welcome Screen: Upon launching Android Studio, you'll be greeted by the Welcome Screen. Here, you can create new projects, open existing ones, access recent projects, and explore various tutorials and resources.

2.2.2 Project Structure: The IDE's main window is divided into several panels:

- **Project Panel:** Displays the file structure of your Android project.
- **Editor Panel:** Where you write and edit code, XML layout files, and other resources.
- **Build Variants Panel:** Allows you to switch between build variants, such as debug and release.
- **Logcat Panel:** Shows real-time logs and debugging information.
- **Gradle Console Panel:** Displays build and sync progress.
- **Toolbar:** Contains buttons for common actions like running your app, syncing the project, and debugging.

2.2.3 Code Editor: Android Studio's code editor provides features like code completion, syntax highlighting, error checking, and code navigation. It supports both Java and Kotlin for Android app development.

2.3 Creating Your First Android Project

Now that you're familiar with Android Studio's interface, it's time to create your first Android project:

2.3.1 New Project Wizard:

- Click on "Start a new Android Studio project" from the Welcome Screen.
- The New Project Wizard will guide you through the project creation process. You'll be prompted to set

project details such as the app's name, package name, and the language (Java or Kotlin).

- You can choose a template that best matches your app's purpose, such as a Blank Activity or a Basic Activity.
- Customize your app's layout and settings, including the target Android version and device orientation.

2.3.2 Project Structure:

- Once your project is created, you'll see the project structure in the Project Panel. This structure includes folders for code, resources, and other assets.

2.3.3 Running Your App:

- Android Studio allows you to run your app on either a physical device or an emulator. Click the "Run" button in the Toolbar, and Android Studio will build and deploy your app to the selected device.

Congratulations! You've successfully created your first Android project in Android Studio. In the following chapters, you'll delve deeper into Android app development, covering topics such as user interface design, coding, testing, and deployment. You'll gradually build your skills to become a proficient Android app developer.

CHAPTER 3: THE ANATOMY OF AN ANDROID APP

In this chapter, we will explore the core components that make up an Android app. Understanding the structure of Android apps is essential for creating effective and user-friendly applications.

3.1 Understanding Activities and Layouts

- **Activities:** In Android, an "Activity" represents a single screen with a user interface. Activities are the building blocks of an Android app and are responsible for interacting with the user. Each app typically consists of multiple activities that users can navigate between. For example, an email app might have separate activities for composing emails, viewing the inbox, and managing settings.

- **Layouts:** Activities are designed using XML layout files. A layout defines the structure and arrangement of UI components (views and widgets) on the screen. Common layout types include RelativeLayout, LinearLayout, and ConstraintLayout. Layouts help ensure that your app's user interface is visually appealing and responsive across various screen sizes and orientations.

3.2 XML Layout Design

- **XML (eXtensible Markup Language):** XML is a markup language used to define the structure and content of Android layout files. XML files are human-readable and describe the arrangement of UI elements within an activity. These files are located in the "res/layout" directory of your Android project.

- **Attributes:** XML layout files use attributes to define properties of UI elements. For example, the "android:id" attribute assigns a unique identifier to a view, making it accessible from the Java or Kotlin code. Other attributes control properties like size, position, and appearance.

Example XML Layout:

```xml
xml
<RelativeLayout
xmlns:android="http://schemas.android.com/apk/res/android"
    xmlns:app="http://schemas.android.com/apk/res-auto"
    xmlns:tools="http://schemas.android.com/tools"
    android:layout_width="match_parent"
    android:layout_height="match_parent"
    tools:context=".MainActivity">

    <TextView
        android:id="@+id/textView"
        android:layout_width="wrap_content"
        android:layout_height="wrap_content"
        android:text="Hello, Android!"
        android:layout_centerInParent="true"/>
```

```
<Button
    android:layout_width="wrap_content"
    android:layout_height="wrap_content"
    android:text="Click Me!"
    android:layout_below="@id/textView"
    android:layout_centerHorizontal="true"
    android:id="@+id/button"/>
```

</RelativeLayout>

3.3 Building User Interfaces with Views and Widgets

- **Views:** Views are the fundamental building blocks of Android user interfaces. Examples of views include TextView (for displaying text), ImageView (for displaying images), EditText (for text input), and Button (for user interaction). Views can be defined in XML layout files and manipulated programmatically in code.

- **Widgets:** Widgets are interactive views that allow users to perform actions or provide input. Examples of widgets include buttons, checkboxes, radio buttons, and seek bars. Widgets are essential for creating dynamic and responsive user interfaces.

Example Usage of Views and Widgets:

```java
// In Java/Kotlin code
TextView textView = findViewById(R.id.textView); // Accessing a TextView by its ID
```

```
Button button = findViewById(R.id.button); // Accessing a Button by
its ID

textView.setText("Welcome to Android!"); // Setting text for a
TextView

button.setOnClickListener(new View.OnClickListener() {
  @Override
  public void onClick(View v) {
    // Define actions to be executed when the button is clicked
    textView.setText("Button Clicked!");
  }
});
```

Understanding how to design layouts using XML, work with views and widgets, and manage activities is fundamental to creating user-friendly Android applications. In the subsequent chapters of this book, we will delve deeper into these concepts and explore more advanced topics in Android app development.

CHAPTER 4: USER INTERACTION AND EVENT HANDLING

User interaction is at the heart of Android app development. In this chapter, we will explore how to handle user input, create interactive UI elements, and manage the state of your user interface to create engaging and responsive Android applications.

4.1 Handling User Input

- **User Input Types:** Android apps can capture various forms of user input, including touch gestures, keyboard input, and voice commands. The primary way to handle user input is through event listeners and callbacks.
- **Event Listeners:** Event listeners are responsible for detecting and responding to user interactions. Common event listeners include OnClickListener for buttons, OnTouchListener for touch events, and TextWatcher for text input.

Example of Handling Button Clicks:

java

```java
Button button = findViewById(R.id.button);

button.setOnClickListener(new View.OnClickListener() {
    @Override
    public void onClick(View v) {
        // Code to execute when the button is clicked
        // For example, you can show a toast message
        Toast.makeText(getApplicationContext(),    "Button    Clicked!",
Toast.LENGTH_SHORT).show();
    }
});
```

4.2 Creating Interactive UI Elements

- **Interactive UI Elements:** To make your app more engaging, you can use interactive UI elements like buttons, checkboxes, radio buttons, and seek bars. These elements allow users to perform actions and provide input.
- **Dialogs:** Dialogs are pop-up windows that can display messages, notifications, or input forms. They are often used to obtain user input or display critical information. Android provides various types of dialogs, including AlertDialogs and DatePickerDialogs.

Example of Using a Checkbox:

```java
java
CheckBox checkBox = findViewById(R.id.checkBox);

checkBox.setOnCheckedChangeListener(new
CompoundButton.OnCheckedChangeListener() {
    @Override
```

20

```
public void onCheckedChanged(CompoundButton buttonView,
boolean isChecked) {
    // Code to execute when the checkbox state changes
    if (isChecked) {
        // Checkbox is checked
        // Perform an action
    } else {
        // Checkbox is unchecked
        // Perform a different action
    }
}
});
```

4.3 Managing UI State

- **UI State:** The state of your app's user interface refers to how the UI elements are displayed and what data they contain. Managing UI state is crucial for providing a seamless user experience.
- **Handling Configuration Changes:** Android devices can change configuration, such as screen orientation (portrait to landscape) or language settings. It's essential to handle these changes properly to avoid data loss and maintain the user's context.
- **Saving and Restoring State:** You can save and restore UI state by using methods like onSaveInstanceState() and onRestoreInstanceState(). These methods allow you to preserve critical data when the app goes through lifecycle changes.

Example of Saving and Restoring UI State:

```java
java
@Override
protected void onSaveInstanceState(Bundle outState) {
    super.onSaveInstanceState(outState);
    // Save important data to the bundle
    outState.putString("key", "value");
}

@Override
protected void onRestoreInstanceState(Bundle savedInstanceState) {
    super.onRestoreInstanceState(savedInstanceState);
    // Restore data from the bundle
    String value = savedInstanceState.getString("key");
    // Update UI elements based on the restored data
}
```

Managing UI state effectively ensures that your app retains its functionality and appearance even when users interact with it in different ways or when the device undergoes changes. It contributes to a smoother user experience and fewer frustrations.

In this chapter, you've learned how to handle user input, create interactive UI elements, and manage the state of your app's user interface. These skills are fundamental for creating Android applications that respond to user actions and provide an engaging user experience. In the following chapters, we'll explore more advanced topics in Android app development.

CHAPTER 5: WORKING WITH INTENTS AND ACTIVITIES

In this chapter, we'll delve into the fundamental concepts of Android app navigation and communication through intents and activities. You'll learn how to move between different screens (activities), pass data between them, and use both explicit and implicit intents to achieve various functionalities.

5.1 Navigating Between Activities

- **Activities as Screens:** In Android, each screen or user interface is represented by an activity. Navigating between activities allows you to transition between different parts of your app's user interface.
- **Intent:** An intent is an abstract description of an operation to be performed. It serves as a message to request an action, such as opening a specific activity or starting a service.
- **Explicit Intent:** An explicit intent explicitly specifies the target component (activity or service) by providing its class name. This is commonly used for navigating between activities within your app.

Example of Starting an Activity with an Explicit Intent:

java
```
Intent intent = new Intent(CurrentActivity.this, TargetActivity.class);
startActivity(intent);
```

5.2 Passing Data Between Activities

- **Data Exchange:** Activities often need to share data, such as user preferences, user inputs, or content between them. Android provides methods for passing data between activities.
- **Using Bundles:** A Bundle is a container for passing data between Android components. You can put various types of data into a bundle and send it along with an intent.

Example of Passing Data Between Activities with an Explicit Intent:

In the sending activity:

java
```
Intent intent = new Intent(CurrentActivity.this, TargetActivity.class);
intent.putExtra("key", "value");
startActivity(intent);
```

In the receiving activity:

java
```
Intent intent = getIntent();
String value = intent.getStringExtra("key");
```

5.3 Using Implicit Intents

- **Implicit Intent:** Unlike explicit intents, implicit intents do not specify the target component by class name. Instead, they define an action or request, and the Android system determines which component should handle it based on the intent's action and data type.
- **Common Uses:** Implicit intents are commonly used for actions like sharing content, opening web pages, making phone calls, sending emails, and accessing device features like the camera.

Example of Using an Implicit Intent to Open a Web Page:

```java
Uri webpage = Uri.parse("https://www.example.com");
Intent intent = new Intent(Intent.ACTION_VIEW, webpage);

// Verify that the intent can be resolved to avoid crashes
if (intent.resolveActivity(getPackageManager()) != null) {
    startActivity(intent);
}
```

Note: Implicit intents rely on the availability of apps that can handle the specified action and data type. If no suitable app is found, the Android system will display an error.

Mastering intents and activities are crucial for building dynamic and interactive Android applications. Whether you're navigating between different screens, passing data between activities, or using implicit intents to access external functionality, these concepts enable you to create apps with rich user experiences and seamless interactions. In the upcoming chapters, we'll explore more advanced topics in Android app development.

CHAPTER 6: DATA STORAGE AND PERSISTENCE

Data storage and persistence are essential aspects of Android app development. In this chapter, we'll explore different methods for storing and managing data in Android applications, including SharedPreferences, SQLite databases, and File I/O.

6.1 Using SharedPreferences

- **SharedPreferences:** SharedPreferences is a simple and lightweight way to store small amounts of key-value pairs of primitive data types. It's commonly used for storing app settings, preferences, and user-specific data.
- **Accessing SharedPreferences:** You can access SharedPreferences through the SharedPreferences class, which is part of the Android framework. Each app has its own set of SharedPreferences that can be accessed using a unique name.

Example of Using SharedPreferences:

```java
// Getting SharedPreferences
```

```java
SharedPreferences                    sharedPreferences              =
getSharedPreferences("MyPrefs", Context.MODE_PRIVATE);

// Writing data to SharedPreferences
SharedPreferences.Editor editor = sharedPreferences.edit();
editor.putString("username", "John");
editor.putInt("highScore", 100);
editor.apply();

// Reading data from SharedPreferences
String username = sharedPreferences.getString("username", "");
int highScore = sharedPreferences.getInt("highScore", 0);
```

6.2 Working with SQLite Databases

- **SQLite Databases:** SQLite is a lightweight, embedded relational database management system included with Android. It's suitable for managing structured data, such as user profiles, lists, and more complex datasets.
- **SQLiteOpenHelper:** To work with SQLite databases, you typically create a subclass of SQLiteOpenHelper. This class helps manage database creation, version management, and opening connections.

Example of Creating and Using an SQLite Database:

```java
java
// Creating a database helper
DatabaseHelper dbHelper = new DatabaseHelper(context);

// Writing data to the database
SQLiteDatabase db = dbHelper.getWritableDatabase();
```

```java
ContentValues values = new ContentValues();
values.put("name", "Alice");
values.put("age", 25);
long newRowId = db.insert("users", null, values);

// Querying data from the database
Cursor cursor = db.query("users", null, null, null, null, null, null);
while (cursor.moveToNext()) {
    String name = cursor.getString(cursor.getColumnIndex("name"));
    int age = cursor.getInt(cursor.getColumnIndex("age"));
    // Process data here
}
cursor.close();
```

6.3 Implementing File I/O

- **File I/O:** Android apps can read from and write to files on the device's internal or external storage. This is useful for storing various types of data, including text files, images, and user-generated content.
- **Permissions:** To access external storage or sensitive data, apps need appropriate permissions declared in the AndroidManifest.xml file and granted by the user.

Example of Writing and Reading Text Files:

```java
java
// Writing to a file
String filename = "myfile.txt";
String fileContents = "Hello, Android!";
try     (FileOutputStream   fos   =     openFileOutput(filename,
Context.MODE_PRIVATE)) {
```

```java
    fos.write(fileContents.getBytes());
}

// Reading from a file
try (FileInputStream fis = openFileInput(filename);
    InputStreamReader isr = new InputStreamReader(fis);
    BufferedReader reader = new BufferedReader(isr)) {
    StringBuilder stringBuilder = new StringBuilder();
    String line;
    while ((line = reader.readLine()) != null) {
        stringBuilder.append(line).append('\n');
    }
    String content = stringBuilder.toString();
    // Process the file content
}
```

Understanding how to use SharedPreferences, SQLite databases, and file I/O is crucial for managing and persisting data in your Android applications. These storage mechanisms provide the flexibility to store and retrieve data according to your app's requirements, whether it's simple preferences, structured data, or user-generated content. In the following chapters, we'll explore more advanced data management techniques and best practices.

CHAPTER 7: NETWORKING AND WEB SERVICES

Networking and web services play a pivotal role in Android app development, allowing your apps to interact with remote servers, retrieve data, and provide dynamic content. In this chapter, we'll explore the process of making HTTP requests using Retrofit, parsing JSON data, and handling network connectivity to create robust and responsive Android applications.

7.1 Making HTTP Requests with Retrofit

- **Retrofit:** Retrofit is a popular and widely used library for making HTTP requests in Android applications. It simplifies the process of creating, sending, and processing HTTP requests by converting HTTP API calls into Java or Kotlin method calls.
- **Retrofit Setup:** To use Retrofit, you need to add the Retrofit library and its dependencies to your app's build.gradle file. You also need to define an interface that specifies the API endpoints and methods for making requests.

Example of Using Retrofit to Make a GET Request:

```java
// Define an interface with API endpoints
public interface ApiService {
    @GET("posts/{id}")
    Call<Post> getPost(@Path("id") int postId);
}

// Create a Retrofit instance
Retrofit retrofit = new Retrofit.Builder()
    .baseUrl("https://jsonplaceholder.typicode.com/")
    .addConverterFactory(GsonConverterFactory.create())
    .build();

// Create an instance of the API interface
ApiService apiService = retrofit.create(ApiService.class);

// Make a GET request
Call<Post> call = apiService.getPost(1);
call.enqueue(new Callback<Post>() {
    @Override
    public void onResponse(Call<Post> call, Response<Post> response)
{
        if (response.isSuccessful()) {
            Post post = response.body();
            // Process the retrieved data
        }
    }

    @Override
    public void onFailure(Call<Post> call, Throwable t) {
        // Handle network errors
    }
});
```

7.2 Parsing JSON Data

- **JSON (JavaScript Object Notation):** JSON is a common data format used for data interchange between a client and a server. Android apps often receive JSON data from web services, and it needs to be parsed into usable objects within your app.
- **Gson:** Gson is a popular JSON parsing library for Android. It allows you to serialize and deserialize JSON data into Java or Kotlin objects seamlessly.

Example of Parsing JSON Data with Gson:

```java
java
// Define a data class that matches the JSON structure
public class Post {
    private int userId;
    private int id;
    private String title;
    private String body;

    // Getters and setters
}

// Parse JSON into a Post object
Gson gson = new Gson();
String json = "{...}"; // Replace with your JSON data
Post post = gson.fromJson(json, Post.class);

// Access data from the Post object
int userId = post.getUserId();
String title = post.getTitle();
```

7.3 Handling Network Connectivity

- **Network Connectivity:** Android devices can be connected to the internet via various networks (Wi-Fi, mobile data, etc.), but network availability is not guaranteed at all times. Handling network connectivity is crucial to ensure your app functions gracefully under different conditions.
- **Connectivity Manager:** The ConnectivityManager class allows you to monitor the network state and type. You can use it to check whether the device is connected to the internet and, if so, what type of network (e.g., Wi-Fi or mobile data) is available.

Example of Checking Network Connectivity:

```java
ConnectivityManager connectivityManager = (ConnectivityManager)
getSystemService(Context.CONNECTIVITY_SERVICE);
NetworkInfo            activeNetwork            =
connectivityManager.getActiveNetworkInfo();

if        (activeNetwork       !=       null        &&
activeNetwork.isConnectedOrConnecting()) {
   if (activeNetwork.getType() == ConnectivityManager.TYPE_WIFI)
{
     // Connected to Wi-Fi
   }       else      if      (activeNetwork.getType()       ==
ConnectivityManager.TYPE_MOBILE) {
     // Connected to mobile data
   }
} else {
   // No network connection
}
```

Properly managing network connectivity ensures that your app responds appropriately to varying network conditions, such as handling offline scenarios or delaying certain actions until a stable connection is available.

Incorporating networking and web services into your Android app opens up a world of possibilities for fetching and sharing data with remote servers. Whether you're retrieving JSON data from an API, sending user data to a server, or handling network connectivity, these skills are essential for creating dynamic and data-driven Android applications. In the following chapters, we'll explore advanced networking concepts and best practices.

CHAPTER 8: USER AUTHENTICATION AND SECURITY

User authentication and security are paramount in Android app development, especially for applications that deal with sensitive user data. This chapter focuses on implementing user authentication, securing user data, and following best practices to ensure the security and privacy of your Android application.

8.1 Implementing User Authentication

User authentication is the process of verifying the identity of a user before granting them access to certain parts of your app or its features. Here are some common methods and considerations for implementing user authentication:

- **Authentication Methods:** Android apps often use various authentication methods, including email/password authentication, social login (e.g., via Google or Facebook), and multi-factor authentication (e.g., SMS codes or biometrics).

- **Firebase Authentication:** Firebase offers a comprehensive authentication system with built-in support for various authentication providers. It simplifies the implementation of user authentication in Android apps.

Example of Implementing Firebase Email/Password Authentication:

```java
java
// Create a Firebase authentication instance
FirebaseAuth mAuth = FirebaseAuth.getInstance();

// Create a new user with email and password
mAuth.createUserWithEmailAndPassword(email, password)
    .addOnCompleteListener(this,                              new
OnCompleteListener<AuthResult>() {
    @Override
    public void onComplete(@NonNull Task<AuthResult> task) {
      if (task.isSuccessful()) {
        // User registration successful
        FirebaseUser user = mAuth.getCurrentUser();
      } else {
        // Registration failed, handle the error
      }
    }
  });
```

8.2 Securing User Data

Securing user data is critical to maintaining user privacy and protecting sensitive information. Consider the following aspects of securing user data in your Android app:

- **Encryption:** Use encryption algorithms to secure data at rest and in transit. For example, use HTTPS for network communication and encrypt sensitive data stored in databases or shared preferences.
- **User Permissions:** Request only the permissions necessary for your app's functionality. Android's permission system helps protect user data by allowing users to grant or deny access to sensitive device features and data.
- **Secure Storage:** Store sensitive data, such as passwords or API keys, securely using Android's KeyStore or other secure storage mechanisms.

8.3 Best Practices for App Security

Ensuring the overall security of your Android app is an ongoing process. Follow these best practices to enhance the security of your application:

- **Keep Libraries Up-to-Date:** Regularly update third-party libraries and dependencies to patch security vulnerabilities.
- **Validate User Inputs:** Always validate user inputs to prevent common security issues like SQL injection and Cross-Site Scripting (XSS) attacks.
- **Implement Session Management:** Manage user sessions securely, and provide mechanisms for users to log out of their accounts.
- **Implement Rate Limiting:** Prevent abuse and brute force attacks by implementing rate limiting on authentication attempts.

- **Implement OAuth2 and Token-based Authentication:** When interacting with third-party APIs, use OAuth2 and token-based authentication to secure API requests.
- **Audit Your Code:** Perform security audits and code reviews to identify and fix potential security vulnerabilities in your codebase.
- **Use Security Headers:** Implement security headers (e.g., Content Security Policy, Cross-Origin Resource Sharing) to protect against common web-based attacks.
- **Implement Secure API Endpoints:** Ensure that your server-side API endpoints are secure and follow best practices for authentication and authorization.
- **Regularly Test for Vulnerabilities:** Use security testing tools and techniques, such as penetration testing and code scanning, to identify and address vulnerabilities.
- **Educate Your Team:** Ensure that your development team is educated about security best practices and follows secure coding guidelines.
- **Respond to Security Incidents:** Have a plan in place to respond to security incidents, such as data breaches or unauthorized access.
- **Comply with Privacy Regulations:** If your app collects and stores user data, ensure compliance with privacy regulations such as GDPR or HIPAA.

By incorporating these best practices into your Android app development process, you can significantly reduce the risk of security vulnerabilities and protect both your users and your app's reputation.

In summary, user authentication and security are critical aspects of Android app development. Implementing strong user authentication, securing user data, and following best practices for app security are essential to building trust with your users and ensuring the privacy and integrity of your application.

CHAPTER 9: BUILDING RESPONSIVE UIS

In this chapter, we'll delve into the intricacies of building responsive user interfaces (UIs) in Android applications. Ensuring that your app remains snappy and responsive is crucial for providing a smooth and enjoyable user experience. We will explore various techniques and tools for achieving this, including threads, AsyncTasks, Loaders, AsyncTaskLoader, and WorkManager.

9.1 Introduction to Threads and AsyncTasks

- **Threads:** Android apps run on a single main thread by default. Lengthy or resource-intensive tasks, such as network requests or database operations, should be moved to background threads to prevent the main thread from becoming unresponsive.
- **AsyncTasks:** AsyncTask is a class that simplifies background thread management. It allows you to perform tasks off the main thread and provides methods for publishing progress and results back to the main thread.

Example of Using AsyncTask:

```java
java
private class MyAsyncTask extends AsyncTask<Void, Integer, String>
{
  @Override
  protected void onPreExecute() {
    // Perform setup tasks before background execution
  }

  @Override
  protected String doInBackground(Void... params) {
    // Perform background tasks here
    return "Result";
  }

  @Override
  protected void onProgressUpdate(Integer... values) {
    // Update UI with progress
  }

  @Override
  protected void onPostExecute(String result) {
    // Update UI with the result
  }
}
```

9.2 Using Loaders and AsyncTaskLoader

- **Loaders:** Loaders are Android components that load data asynchronously and automatically manage the lifecycle of background tasks. They are particularly useful for loading data from databases or content providers.

42

- **AsyncTaskLoader:** AsyncTaskLoader is an extension of the Loader class that simplifies background loading of data with AsyncTask. It addresses issues related to configuration changes, ensuring data is retained during screen rotations.

Example of Using AsyncTaskLoader:

```java
java
public class MyLoader extends AsyncTaskLoader<List<Data>> {
    public MyLoader(Context context) {
        super(context);
    }

    @Override
    public List<Data> loadInBackground() {
        // Load and return data in the background
        return fetchData();
    }

    @Override
    protected void onStartLoading() {
        forceLoad();
    }
}
```

9.3 Handling Background Tasks with WorkManager

- **WorkManager:** WorkManager is a library for scheduling and executing background tasks in a way that is efficient and compatible with various Android versions. It allows you to define tasks that can run immediately or with specified constraints, such as network availability or charging status.

Example of Using WorkManager to Schedule a Task:

```java
// Create a OneTimeWorkRequest
OneTimeWorkRequest workRequest = new
OneTimeWorkRequest.Builder(MyWorker.class).build();

// Schedule the work request
WorkManager.getInstance(context).enqueue(workRequest);
```

- **Worker:** A Worker is a class that defines the actual work to be done in the background. You can customize it to perform tasks like data synchronization, periodic updates, or file uploads.

```java
public class MyWorker extends Worker {
    public MyWorker(
        @NonNull Context context,
        @NonNull WorkerParameters params) {
        super(context, params);
    }

    @NonNull
    @Override
    public Result doWork() {
        // Perform background work here
        return Result.success();
    }
}
```

Building responsive UIs in Android is essential for providing a seamless and enjoyable user experience. By offloading time-consuming tasks to background threads or using tools like AsyncTask, Loaders, AsyncTaskLoader, and WorkManager, you can keep your app responsive and prevent it from freezing or crashing when handling resource-intensive operations. These techniques ensure that users can interact with your app smoothly, even when performing complex tasks.

CHAPTER 10: MULTIMEDIA AND CAMERA INTEGRATION

Multimedia and camera integration are essential aspects of modern Android applications. This chapter explores various multimedia-related topics, including working with images and bitmaps, implementing audio and video playback, and integrating the camera for image capture.

10.1 Working with Images and Bitmaps

- **Bitmap:** A Bitmap is a representation of an image in Android. It is a pixel-based graphic that can be displayed in image views or used in various UI components.
- **Image Loading Libraries:** To efficiently load and display images in Android apps, developers often use image loading libraries like Picasso, Glide, or Coil. These libraries handle caching, resizing, and displaying images while minimizing memory usage.

Example of Loading and Displaying an Image with Picasso:

```java
String imageUrl = "https://www.example.com/image.jpg";
ImageView imageView = findViewById(R.id.imageView);

Picasso.get().load(imageUrl).into(imageView);
```

- **Bitmap Processing:** You can perform various image operations on bitmaps, such as cropping, rotating, and applying filters or transformations.

10.2 Implementing Audio and Video Playback

- **Audio and Video Playback:** Android provides MediaPlayer for audio and video playback. It supports a wide range of audio and video formats. You can create a MediaPlayer instance, set the data source (e.g., a URL or local file), and control playback (start, pause, stop, etc.).

Example of Audio Playback with MediaPlayer:

```java
MediaPlayer mediaPlayer = MediaPlayer.create(this, R.raw.audio_file);
mediaPlayer.start();
```

- **Video Playback:** VideoView is a UI component for displaying videos. It simplifies video playback by handling many of the details associated with displaying video content.

Example of Video Playback with VideoView:

```java
```

```java
VideoView videoView = findViewById(R.id.videoView);
videoView.setVideoURI(Uri.parse("https://www.example.com/video.m
p4"));
videoView.start();
```

10.3 Integrating the Camera and Image Capture

- **Camera Integration:** Android devices often come equipped with one or more cameras. Integrating the device's camera into your app allows users to capture photos or record videos directly from your app's interface.
- **Camera API:** Android offers two APIs for camera integration: Camera1 API (deprecated but still supported) and Camera2 API (recommended for modern apps). Camera2 API provides more control and flexibility over camera features and settings.

Example of Capturing an Image with Camera2 API:

```java
java
// Set up a camera manager and camera capture session
CameraManager      cameraManager      =      (CameraManager)
getSystemService(Context.CAMERA_SERVICE);
cameraManager.openCamera(cameraId,                          new
CameraDevice.StateCallback() {
    @Override
    public void onOpened(@NonNull CameraDevice camera) {
        // Camera is opened; create a capture session
        // Configure and create a capture request
        // Start the image capture process
    }

    @Override
```

```java
public void onDisconnected(@NonNull CameraDevice camera) {
    // Handle camera disconnection
}

@Override
public void onError(@NonNull CameraDevice camera, int error) {
    // Handle camera errors
}
}, null);
```

- **Image Capture:** After configuring the camera and capturing an image, you can save the image to the device's storage or process it within your app.

Example of Saving Captured Image to Storage:

```java
java
// Capture an image and save it to a file
imageReader.setOnImageAvailableListener(new
ImageReader.OnImageAvailableListener() {
    @Override
    public void onImageAvailable(ImageReader reader) {
        Image image = reader.acquireLatestImage();
        // Process the image or save it to storage
        image.close();
    }
}, null);
```

Multimedia elements, such as images, audio, and video, are powerful tools for enhancing the user experience in Android apps. By learning how to work with images and bitmaps, implement audio and video playback, and integrate the camera for image capture, you can create rich and engaging applications that leverage multimedia content effectively. These capabilities allow you to create apps that cater to a wide range of user needs and preferences.

CHAPTER 11: LOCATION-BASED SERVICES

Location-based services (LBS) are integral to many Android applications, enabling features like mapping, navigation, location-aware content, and more. In this chapter, we'll explore how to use the Location API to access device location data, implement maps and location-based features, and leverage geofencing and location awareness to create context-aware apps.

11.1 Using the Location API

- **Location API:** Android provides the Location API to access the device's location information, including latitude, longitude, altitude, and accuracy. It allows you to retrieve the device's current location, monitor location changes, and request location updates.
- **Location Providers:** The Location API supports various location providers, including GPS, network, and passive providers. GPS provides high-accuracy location data but may drain the battery, while

network providers use cellular and Wi-Fi signals for approximate location information.

Example of Requesting Location Updates:

```java
LocationManager locationManager = (LocationManager) getSystemService(Context.LOCATION_SERVICE);
LocationListener locationListener = new LocationListener() {
    @Override
    public void onLocationChanged(Location location) {
        // Handle location updates
        double latitude = location.getLatitude();
        double longitude = location.getLongitude();
    }

    // Other callback methods for status changes and provider availability
};

// Request location updates
locationManager.requestLocationUpdates(LocationManager.GPS_PROVIDER, 0, 0, locationListener);
```

11.2 Implementing Maps and Location-Based Features

- **Google Maps:** Google Maps is a powerful tool for implementing maps and location-based features in Android apps. You can integrate Google Maps by using the Google Maps Android API, which provides various features like map display, geocoding, and route calculation.
- **Markers and Overlays:** You can add markers, polygons, polylines, and other overlays to maps to

visualize location-based data or provide interactive elements for users.

Example of Adding a Marker to a Google Map:

```java
GoogleMap googleMap = ((SupportMapFragment) getSupportFragmentManager().findFragmentById(R.id.map)).getMap();
LatLng location = new LatLng(37.7749, -122.4194);
MarkerOptions markerOptions = new MarkerOptions().position(location).title("San Francisco");
googleMap.addMarker(markerOptions);
```

- **Location-Based Features:** Location-based features can include location-aware recommendations, nearby points of interest (POIs), and real-time navigation. These features rely on the user's current or specified location to provide relevant information and functionality.

11.3 Geofencing and Location Awareness

- **Geofencing:** Geofencing involves defining virtual boundaries (geofences) around real-world geographic areas. When a user's device enters or exits a geofence, the app can trigger specific actions or notifications. Geofencing is valuable for location-based marketing, safety alerts, and context-aware experiences.

- **Location Awareness:** Location-aware apps can adapt their behavior based on the user's location.

For example, an app can provide different content or functionality when the user is at home, work, or a shopping mall. Location awareness relies on continuously monitoring the user's location and applying predefined rules or contexts.

Example of Geofencing Implementation:

```java
Geofence.Builder builder = new Geofence.Builder();
builder.setCircularRegion(latitude, longitude, radius);
builder.setExpirationDuration(Geofence.NEVER_EXPIRE);
builder.setTransitionTypes(Geofence.GEOFENCE_TRANSITION_EN
TER | Geofence.GEOFENCE_TRANSITION_EXIT);

Geofence geofence = builder.build();

GeofencingRequest.Builder        requestBuilder        =        new
GeofencingRequest.Builder();
requestBuilder.addGeofence(geofence);

PendingIntent pendingIntent = PendingIntent.getBroadcast(context, 0,
new                          Intent("GEOFENCE_ACTION"),
PendingIntent.FLAG_UPDATE_CURRENT);

LocationServices.getGeofencingClient(context).addGeofences(request
Builder.build(), pendingIntent);
```

Location-based services empower Android apps to offer personalized, location-aware experiences and interact with the real world in new and exciting ways. Whether you're building mapping applications, geofencing solutions, or location-aware content, mastering location-based services can greatly enhance the value and utility of your Android applications.

CHAPTER 12: PUBLISHING YOUR APP

Publishing your Android app is the culmination of your development efforts. In this chapter, we will explore the steps required to prepare your app for release, generate signed APKs (Android Package files), and upload your app to the Google Play Store, one of the most popular app distribution platforms.

12.1 Preparing Your App for Release

Before you publish your app, you need to ensure it's ready for a wider audience. Here are some key steps to prepare your app for release:

- **Testing:** Thoroughly test your app to identify and fix any bugs or issues. Ensure that it works well on various devices, screen sizes, and Android versions.

- **Performance Optimization:** Optimize your app's performance, including reducing memory usage, improving startup times, and minimizing battery consumption.
- **User Experience:** Ensure that the app provides a seamless and user-friendly experience. Test the app's navigation, UI design, and responsiveness.
- **Compliance:** Review and comply with Google Play Store policies and guidelines, including content guidelines, age rating, and payment processing.
- **Localization:** If your app targets a global audience, consider localizing it by translating text and adapting content to different languages and regions.
- **Privacy and Security:** Protect user data and ensure that your app follows privacy best practices. Use secure communication protocols and handle sensitive information securely.
- **App Icons and Graphics:** Create high-quality app icons and graphics that represent your app well. Visual appeal can significantly impact app downloads.

12.2 Generating Signed APKs

Before you can publish your app, you need to generate signed APKs. This involves signing your app with a digital certificate, which verifies the app's authenticity and ensures that updates can be installed over the existing version.

- **Key Generation:** Use Android's keytool or a keystore management tool to generate a keystore file and key pair.
- **Signing APKs:** Sign your app's APKs using the generated keystore file. You can do this using Android Studio's Gradle signing configuration or by using command-line tools.

Example of Signing APKs with Gradle in build.gradle:

```gradle
android {
  signingConfigs {
    release {
        storeFile file('your-keystore-file.jks')
        storePassword 'your-keystore-password'
        keyAlias 'your-key-alias'
        keyPassword 'your-key-password'
    }
  }
  buildTypes {
    release {
        signingConfig signingConfigs.release
        // Other release-specific configurations
    }
  }
}
```

12.3 Uploading to the Google Play Store

Once you have prepared your app and generated signed APKs, you can proceed to upload it to the Google Play Store:

- **Create a Developer Account:** If you don't already have one, create a Google Play Developer account. There is a one-time registration fee.
- **App Listing:** Fill in all the required information for your app's listing, including the app's title, description, screenshots, icons, and other assets. Write an engaging app description and choose relevant keywords for discoverability.
- **Pricing and Distribution:** Decide whether your app will be free or paid. Set pricing details if applicable. Choose the countries and regions where your app will be available.
- **Content Rating:** Provide content ratings for your app based on Google's guidelines. This helps ensure your app is suitable for different age groups.
- **APK Upload:** Upload the signed APKs and specify which version of the app you are uploading (e.g., Alpha, Beta, Production).
- **Publish:** Submit your app for review. Google will review your app to ensure it complies with their policies. Once approved, you can publish it to the Play Store.
- **Updates:** You can release updates to your app at any time by uploading new APKs. Users who have the app installed will receive notifications about updates.
- **Promotion:** Promote your app using various strategies, such as app store optimization (ASO), social media, online advertising, and user engagement campaigns.

Remember that the app publishing process may take some time, especially during the review phase. Google Play Store provides a wealth of resources and guidelines to help you navigate the publishing process and promote your app effectively.

Publishing your Android app is a significant milestone. By thoroughly preparing your app, generating signed APKs, and following Google's guidelines, you can make your app available to a global audience on the Google Play Store and potentially reach millions of users.

CHAPTER 13: MONETIZATION AND IN-APP PURCHASES

Monetization is a crucial aspect of app development, as it allows you to generate revenue from your Android application. In this chapter, we'll explore various monetization options, including in-app purchases and ad integration with AdMob.

13.1 Exploring Monetization Options

There are several monetization strategies you can consider for your Android app. The choice of strategy depends on your app's nature, target audience, and goals. Here are some common monetization options:

- **Free with Ads:** Offer your app for free and generate revenue by displaying advertisements to users. You can use ad networks like AdMob to serve ads in your app.
- **Freemium Model:** Provide a free version of your app with limited features and offer premium or ad-free versions for a fee. Users can upgrade through in-app purchases.
- **In-App Purchases:** Allow users to purchase digital goods or premium features within your app. This is commonly used for games, subscriptions, or unlocking additional content.
- **Subscription Model:** Charge users a recurring fee to access premium content or features. Subscriptions can provide a steady stream of revenue.
- **Paid Apps:** Sell your app directly on the Google Play Store for a one-time purchase price. Users pay to download and use the app without any additional charges.
- **Sponsorships and Partnerships:** Partner with other businesses to promote their products or services within your app. This can include sponsored content, product placements, or affiliate marketing.

13.2 Implementing In-App Purchases

In-app purchases (IAPs) enable users to buy digital items, services, or premium features within your app. Here are the key steps to implement in-app purchases:

- **Set Up a Merchant Account:** You'll need a Google Play Console account and a merchant account to handle payments.
- **Integrate Billing Library:** Use Google's Billing Library to handle the purchasing flow, manage product catalogs, and handle transactions.
- **Create In-App Products:** Define the digital items or features that users can purchase within your app. Configure their prices and descriptions on the Google Play Console.
- **Implement Purchase Flow:** Implement the purchase flow in your app, allowing users to browse and buy in-app products.
- **Handle Transactions:** Use the Billing Library to handle transactions, verify purchases, and unlock premium content or features for users who make purchases.
- **Testing:** Test in-app purchases thoroughly using test accounts to ensure the purchasing flow works correctly.

13.3 Ad Integration with AdMob

AdMob is Google's advertising platform for mobile apps. It allows you to monetize your Android app by displaying ads from various sources, including Google AdMob, Ad

Manager, and third-party ad networks. Here's how to integrate AdMob into your app:

- **Set Up an AdMob Account:** Create an AdMob account and link it to your Google Play Console account.
- **Create Ad Units:** Define ad units in AdMob, such as banner ads, interstitial ads, or rewarded ads. Each ad unit has a unique identifier that you'll use in your app.
- **Integrate AdMob SDK:** Add the AdMob SDK to your app's build.gradle file and initialize it in your app code.
- **Load and Display Ads:** Use the AdMob SDK to load and display ads in your app's user interface. You can specify where and how ads should appear.
- **Ad Formats:** AdMob supports various ad formats, including banner ads, native ads, video ads, and rewarded ads. Choose the ad formats that fit your app's design and user experience.
- **Ad Mediation:** Implement ad mediation to maximize your ad revenue. Ad mediation allows you to serve ads from multiple ad networks to optimize fill rates and eCPM (effective cost per mille).
- **Testing:** Test ad integration thoroughly to ensure ads are displayed correctly and comply with AdMob's policies.

Monetization through in-app purchases and ad integration can provide a sustainable source of revenue for your Android app. However, it's essential to strike a balance between monetization and user experience to avoid alienating your user base. By offering value to your users and providing a seamless monetization experience, you can maximize your app's revenue potential while maintaining user satisfaction.

CHAPTER 14: TESTING AND DEBUGGING

Testing and debugging are critical phases in Android app development to ensure that your app functions correctly and delivers a smooth user experience. In this chapter, we'll explore various types of testing, debugging techniques, and tools, as well as the importance of beta testing and gathering user feedback.

14.1 Types of Testing (Unit, UI, Integration)

Testing is an integral part of the app development process. Different types of testing serve various purposes, and a combination of these tests ensures the reliability and quality of your app. Here are three essential types of testing in Android app development:

- **Unit Testing:**
  - **Purpose:** Unit testing focuses on testing individual components or functions in isolation. It helps ensure that each unit of code works correctly and produces the expected output.
  - **Tools:** JUnit and AndroidJUnit are commonly used for unit testing in Android. Mockito and Espresso can help with mocking and UI testing, respectively.
  - **Example:** Testing a function that calculates the total price of items in a shopping cart.
- **UI Testing:**
  - **Purpose:** UI testing verifies that the user interface and interactions with the app function correctly. It helps catch issues related to user experience and visual elements.
  - **Tools:** Espresso is a popular framework for UI testing in Android. UI Automator is

another option for testing interactions across app components.

- o **Example:** Ensuring that tapping a button opens a new activity or that scrolling a list displays the expected data.

- **Integration Testing:**
  - o **Purpose:** Integration testing validates the interactions and dependencies between different parts of your app, including services, components, and external APIs.
  - o **Tools:** Robolectric and TestContainers are useful for running integration tests in Android.
  - o **Example:** Testing how different app modules work together, such as verifying that data retrieved from a web API is displayed correctly in the app's UI.

14.2 Debugging Techniques and Tools

Debugging is the process of identifying and fixing issues or bugs in your app's code. Effective debugging can save you a significant amount of time and frustration during development. Here are some debugging techniques and tools:

- **Logcat:** Use Android's Logcat tool to view logs generated by your app. You can add log statements to your code to track the flow and variables' values.
- **Breakpoints:** Set breakpoints in your code using Android Studio's debugger. This allows you to

pause execution and inspect variables and the call stack.

- **Inspect Variables:** Android Studio's debugger provides a powerful variable inspector to examine the values of variables during execution.
- **Profiling Tools:** Utilize Android Profiler to analyze your app's performance, memory usage, and CPU utilization. This can help identify bottlenecks and memory leaks.
- **Exception Handling:** Implement exception handling in your code to gracefully handle errors and prevent crashes. Catch and log exceptions to understand the root causes of issues.
- **Remote Debugging:** Debug apps running on physical devices by connecting them to your development machine via USB and using Android Studio. You can also use remote debugging with emulator instances.

14.3 Beta Testing and User Feedback

Beta testing is a crucial phase in the app development process that allows you to gather feedback from real users before releasing your app to the public. Here's how to approach beta testing:

- **Closed Beta Testing:** Invite a select group of users, such as friends, colleagues, or a specific user segment, to test your app. Use Google Play's closed beta testing feature to distribute the app to these testers.

- **Feedback Collection:** Encourage beta testers to provide feedback on their experiences with your app. Create a feedback channel or use platforms like Google Play Console to collect comments, bug reports, and suggestions.
- **Iterative Development:** Act on the feedback received from beta testers by addressing reported issues and implementing suggested improvements. Beta testing is an excellent opportunity to refine your app before its public release.
- **Open Beta Testing:** Once you've addressed major issues identified during closed beta testing, consider conducting open beta testing. This involves making your app available to a broader audience.
- **User Feedback Loop:** Continuously engage with your app's users, both during beta testing and after the public release. Listen to their feedback, implement improvements, and maintain a positive feedback loop to build a loyal user base.

Testing and debugging are ongoing processes throughout your app's lifecycle. Regularly test new features and updates, gather user feedback, and use debugging tools to ensure your app is reliable, performs well, and delivers an excellent user experience. By investing time in testing and debugging, you can create a polished and successful Android app.

CHAPTER 15: OPTIMIZATION AND PERFORMANCE

Optimizing the performance of your Android app is crucial to ensure that it runs smoothly, uses resources efficiently, and provides a satisfying user experience. In this chapter, we'll explore techniques for profiling your app, optimizing memory and CPU usage, and best practices for app performance.

15.1 Profiling Your App

Profiling your app involves analyzing its behavior, resource utilization, and bottlenecks to identify areas that need improvement. Here's how you can profile your app:

- **Performance Profilers:** Android Studio provides built-in performance profilers for CPU, memory, and network usage. These profilers help you visualize your app's behavior and identify performance issues.
- **Systrace:** Systrace is a powerful tool that captures detailed system-level performance data, including CPU, GPU, and I/O activity. It can help pinpoint performance bottlenecks and issues in your app.
- **Memory Profiling:** Use Android Studio's Memory Profiler to monitor your app's memory usage. Identify memory leaks, inefficient memory allocation, and unnecessary objects that can cause performance degradation.
- **Network Profiling:** Profiling network requests can help you optimize data transfer and reduce latency. Tools like Network Profiler in Android Studio provide insights into network activity.
- **UI Rendering Profiling:** UI rendering can affect app performance. Tools like Layout Inspector and GPU Profiler in Android Studio help analyze and optimize UI rendering performance.

15.2 Optimizing Memory and CPU Usage

Optimizing memory and CPU usage is critical for delivering a responsive and efficient app. Here are some strategies to optimize these resources:

- **Memory Optimization:**
  - o **Avoid Memory Leaks:** Carefully manage object references to prevent memory leaks. Use weak references when necessary, and be mindful of long-lived objects.
  - o **Use Efficient Data Structures:** Choose data structures that minimize memory usage. Consider using SparseArray for sparse data and avoid unnecessary object creation.
  - o **Recycle Bitmaps:** Recycle Bitmaps when they are no longer needed to free up memory. Use BitmapFactory.Options to load scaled-down images.
  - o **Memory Caching:** Implement memory caching for frequently used data to reduce disk I/O and improve performance.
- **CPU Optimization:**
  - o **Background Threads:** Offload CPU-intensive tasks to background threads to keep the main UI thread responsive. Use AsyncTask, Thread, or Kotlin Coroutines for background processing.
  - o **Multithreading:** Use multithreading and parallel processing for CPU-bound tasks, but be cautious of thread synchronization issues.

- o **UI Rendering Optimization:** Minimize complex layout hierarchies and use efficient drawing techniques to reduce CPU usage during UI rendering.
- o **Reduce CPU Wake Locks:** Avoid keeping the CPU awake unnecessarily by releasing wake locks when they are no longer needed.
- o **Battery Optimization:** Implement background processing judiciously to conserve battery life. Use WorkManager for efficient scheduling of background tasks.

15.3 Best Practices for App Performance

To ensure optimal app performance, follow these best practices:

- **Minimize App Size:** Reduce the size of your app's APK by removing unused resources, optimizing images, and using ProGuard or R8 for code shrinking and obfuscation.
- **Optimize Startup Time:** Minimize the time it takes for your app to launch by initializing only essential components during startup. Use techniques like lazy loading and preloading.
- **Use Efficient Algorithms:** Choose efficient algorithms and data structures for data manipulation and processing.
- **Implement Caching:** Cache data and resources to reduce network requests and improve response times.

- **Network Optimization:** Use appropriate caching headers, compress responses, and handle network failures gracefully to ensure a smooth network experience.
- **Regularly Test on Real Devices:** Test your app on a variety of real Android devices with different screen sizes, hardware configurations, and Android versions to ensure compatibility and performance.
- **Performance Monitoring:** Implement performance monitoring tools like Firebase Performance Monitoring to track and analyze app performance in production.
- **User Feedback:** Listen to user feedback and use analytics tools to identify performance issues experienced by users.
- **Continuous Optimization:** Performance optimization is an ongoing process. Regularly revisit your app's performance metrics, profile for issues, and optimize as needed, especially after introducing new features or updates.

Optimizing your Android app's performance is essential to provide a seamless user experience and maintain user satisfaction. By profiling your app, optimizing memory and CPU usage, and following best practices, you can create an app that is fast, responsive, and efficient on a wide range of Android devices.

APPENDIX A: SAMPLE APP PROJECT

In this appendix, we'll guide you through the process of building a practical Android app from scratch. This project will provide a step-by-step code walkthrough, helping you understand the development process and common issues you might encounter.

Building a Practical Android App from Scratch

Step 1: Project Planning

- Define the app's purpose, target audience, and core features.
- Create wireframes or sketches to visualize the app's user interface.
- Decide on the app's architecture and the technologies you'll use (e.g., Kotlin, Android Jetpack).

Step 2: Setting Up the Development Environment

- Install Android Studio and set up the Android SDK.
- Create a new Android project, selecting the appropriate project template (e.g., Empty Activity, Bottom Navigation Activity).

Step 3: Designing the User Interface (UI)

- Use XML layout files to design the app's UI, including activities, fragments, and views.
- Apply best practices for responsive design, considering various screen sizes and orientations.

Step 4: Implementing Functionality

- Write Kotlin or Java code to add functionality to your app's UI elements.

- Implement user interactions, navigation, data retrieval, and storage.

Step 5: Testing and Debugging

- Conduct unit testing, UI testing, and integration testing to identify and fix bugs.
- Use Android Studio's debugging tools to diagnose issues and optimize code.

Step 6: Performance Optimization

- Profile your app to identify bottlenecks and optimize memory and CPU usage.
- Implement best practices for performance, such as background processing and lazy loading.

Step 7: Testing on Real Devices

- Test your app on a variety of physical devices and emulators.
- Ensure compatibility with different Android versions and screen sizes.

Step 8: Deployment

- Generate signed APKs for production.
- Create an app listing on the Google Play Store, including descriptions, screenshots, and promotional materials.

- Publish your app to the Google Play Store and monitor user feedback.

Step-by-Step Code Walkthrough

Throughout the development process, we'll provide code examples and explanations for each step. You'll learn how to create activities, fragments, handle user input, fetch data from web services, and more. The code walkthrough will cover essential Android development concepts, including:

- Layout design using XML.
- Activity and Fragment lifecycles.
- Event handling and user input.
- Data binding and data storage.
- Networking and API integration.
- User interface design principles.
- Performance optimization techniques.

Troubleshooting Common Issues

Android development can come with its share of challenges. In this appendix, we'll address common issues that developers often encounter, such as:

- App crashes and error messages.
- UI layout problems and design inconsistencies.
- Debugging and diagnosing issues using Android Studio's tools.
- Handling different screen sizes and orientations.
- Performance bottlenecks and memory management.

- Compatibility and testing across multiple Android versions and devices.

By following the sample app project, you'll gain practical experience in Android app development, learn valuable troubleshooting techniques, and build a strong foundation for creating your own Android applications. This hands-on approach will help you apply the concepts and skills covered in the main chapters of this book to real-world app development scenarios.

APPENDIX B: ANDROID DEVELOPMENT TIPS AND TRICKS

In this appendix, we'll provide a collection of Android development tips and tricks that can enhance your productivity, streamline your debugging process, and optimize your app's performance. These tips cover a wide range of topics, from useful shortcuts and techniques to debugging strategies and performance optimization guidelines.

Handy Shortcuts and Techniques

1. **Android Studio Shortcuts:**
   - Learn essential keyboard shortcuts in Android Studio to navigate, refactor, and debug your code efficiently. For example, Ctrl/Cmd + Click to jump to a declaration, Alt + Enter for quick fixes, and Shift + Shift for quick search.
2. **Code Templates and Live Templates:**
   - Create custom code templates and live templates in Android Studio to automate repetitive coding tasks. For example, you can create templates for generating common code patterns like RecyclerView adapters or Parcelable implementations.
3. **Code Folding:**
   - Use code folding to hide sections of code that you don't need to see while working on specific parts of your project. This makes your code more manageable, especially in large files.
4. **Version Control Integration:**
   - Learn how to use the built-in version control tools in Android Studio (e.g., Git) to track changes, collaborate with others, and manage your project's history.

5. **Custom Code Styles:**
    - o Define custom code styles and formatting rules to enforce consistent coding standards across your project. This helps make your code more readable and maintainable.

Debugging Tips

1. **Conditional Breakpoints:**
    - o Use conditional breakpoints to break the debugger's execution when specific conditions are met. This can be incredibly useful for tracking down issues in loops or complex logic.
2. **Evaluate Expressions:**
    - o Android Studio allows you to evaluate expressions and variables while debugging. This can help you inspect values and quickly understand what's happening in your code.
3. **Logcat Filters:**
    - o Set up Logcat filters to focus on specific types of log messages (e.g., errors, warnings) or to filter by tag. This can help you pinpoint issues more efficiently.
4. **Memory Profiler:**
    - o Use the Memory Profiler in Android Studio to identify memory leaks and optimize memory usage in your app.
5. **Crashlytics and Analytics:**

- o Implement crash reporting and analytics tools (e.g., Firebase Crashlytics, Google Analytics) to track and analyze issues and user behavior in your app, even in production.

Performance Optimization Tips

1. **AsyncTask vs. Kotlin Coroutines:**
   - o Consider migrating from AsyncTask to Kotlin Coroutines for handling background tasks. Coroutines provide more concise and efficient asynchronous programming.
2. **RecyclerView Optimization:**
   - o Optimize RecyclerView performance by implementing efficient ViewHolders, using DiffUtil for data updates, and employing pagination for large data sets.
3. **Bitmap Handling:**
   - o When working with images, use libraries like Glide or Picasso to efficiently load and cache bitmaps, reducing memory usage and improving app performance.
4. **Network Requests:**
   - o Make network requests efficiently by using libraries like Retrofit for REST APIs. Implement caching, handle network errors gracefully, and avoid unnecessary requests.
5. **ProGuard/R8 Obfuscation:**

- o Enable ProGuard or R8 obfuscation to obfuscate your code before release, making it more challenging for reverse engineering and reducing APK size.

6. **Background Processing:**
   - o Offload CPU-intensive tasks to background threads or services to keep the main UI thread responsive. Consider using WorkManager for scheduled tasks.

7. **UI Rendering Performance:**
   - o Optimize UI rendering by reducing the complexity of layout hierarchies, using ConstraintLayout for responsive designs, and minimizing overdraw.

8. **Database Optimization:**
   - o Optimize database performance by using appropriate indexes, executing queries in background threads, and using Room's built-in support for LiveData.

These Android development tips and tricks can help you become a more efficient and proficient developer. By incorporating these techniques into your workflow, you'll be better equipped to create high-quality Android apps that perform well and provide a great user experience.

APPENDIX C: GLOSSARY

This glossary provides key Android development terminology and their definitions, helping you better understand the concepts and jargon commonly used in Android app development.

Activity: An Activity is a fundamental component of an Android app that represents a single screen with a user interface. It can be thought of as a window where the user interacts with the app.

Android Debug Bridge (ADB): A command-line tool used for communication between a development machine and an Android device or emulator. ADB allows developers to install, debug, and interact with Android devices.

API (Application Programming Interface): An API defines a set of rules and protocols that enable different software applications to communicate with each other. In Android, APIs provide access to the platform's features and functionalities.

APK (Android Package): An APK is the file format used to distribute and install Android apps. It contains the app's code, resources, manifest file, and other essential assets.

Dex (Dalvik Executable): A file format used by the Android runtime (formerly Dalvik) to execute compiled Android app code. It's generated from Java bytecode during the build process.

Fragment: A Fragment is a modular and reusable portion of an Android UI that can be combined with other fragments to create a multi-pane user interface, making it suitable for different device screen sizes and orientations.

Gradle: A build automation tool used in Android development to manage dependencies, build APKs, and perform various build-related tasks. It uses Groovy or Kotlin DSL for configuration.

Intent: An Intent is an abstract description of an operation to be performed, such as starting an activity, broadcasting a message, or invoking a service. It serves as a message passed between Android components.

Manifest File: The AndroidManifest.xml file contains essential information about an Android app, including its package name, permissions, activities, services, and receivers. It serves as a blueprint for the app's structure.

Layout: A layout defines the structure and arrangement of UI components in an Android app. It can be created using XML files or programmatically.

Material Design: Google's design language for creating visually appealing and consistent user interfaces across Android devices. Material Design emphasizes elements like cards, animations, and responsive layouts.

RecyclerView: A UI component used for displaying large sets of data in a scrollable list or grid format. It recycles view items to minimize memory usage and improve performance.

SDK (Software Development Kit): An SDK is a set of tools, libraries, and documentation that allows developers to create software applications for a specific platform. In

Android development, the Android SDK provides the necessary resources for building Android apps.

View: A View is a fundamental UI component in Android that represents a user interface element, such as a button, text field, or image. Views can be organized into layouts to create the app's user interface.

XML (Extensible Markup Language): A markup language used for describing data and its structure. In Android, XML is commonly used for defining UI layouts and storing configuration files.

This glossary provides a foundation for understanding key Android development concepts and terminology. As you delve deeper into Android app development, you'll encounter additional terms and concepts that will contribute to your proficiency in building Android applications.

APPENDIX D: INDEX

The index is a comprehensive reference guide that helps readers quickly locate specific topics, concepts, and terms within a book. In the context of this Android app development guide, the index serves as a valuable tool for finding relevant information and navigating the content effectively. Here's an explanation of how the index works and its importance:

How the Index Works:

1. **Alphabetical Listing:** The index is organized alphabetically, with entries listed in ascending order from A to Z. Each entry represents a term, topic, or concept covered in the book.
2. **Page References:** Next to each indexed term, you'll find page numbers that indicate where in the book the term is discussed. These page references help readers locate the information they need.
3. **Subentries:** Some indexed terms may have subentries to further categorize or specify the topic. Subentries are typically indented beneath the main entry and may have their page references.

The Importance of the Index:

1. **Quick Reference:** The index allows readers to quickly locate specific information within the book without having to read it cover-to-cover. This is especially valuable when you want to revisit a particular concept or troubleshoot a specific issue.
2. **Efficient Navigation:** In a comprehensive guide like this one, the index streamlines navigation and helps readers jump directly to the relevant sections, saving time and effort.

3. **Comprehensive Coverage:** A well-constructed index ensures that all key topics and terms are included, ensuring that readers can find the information they need, even if they're not familiar with the book's structure or organization.

How to Use the Index:

To utilize the index effectively, follow these steps:

1. **Locate the Index:** The index is typically found at the end of the book, often after the appendices or glossary.
2. **Search for Keywords:** Identify the keyword or term you're interested in. Scan the index to find where it's listed alphabetically.
3. **Check Page References:** Once you've found the keyword or term, check the page references listed alongside it. These page numbers indicate where you can find detailed information about the topic.
4. **Navigate to the Pages:** Turn to the pages listed in the index to access the content related to the keyword or term you're interested in.